And the glory of God shone around them.

ADVENT DEVOTIONAL

DR. BRIAN SIMMONS with JEREMY BOUMA

BroadStreet
PUBLISHING

Published by BroadStreet Publishing Group, LLC
Savage, Minnesota, USA
www.broadstreetpublishing.com

AND THE GLORY OF GOD SHONE AROUND THEM

Advent Devotional

By Dr. Brian Simmons with Jeremy Bouma

Inspired by *The Passion Translation* by Dr. Brian Simmons
www.thepassiontranslation.com

978-1-4245-6251-0 (paperback)

Design by Garborg Design Works, Inc. | www.garborgdesign.com

Printed in the USA.

20 21 22 23 24 5 4 3 2 1

CONTENTS

INTRODUCTION

I just love the Christmas season! Do you?

What I love even more is the story behind the season, the story of Jesus—the reason for the season, as they say. This is why I'm thrilled to share with you these twenty-one devotionals. Each one is inspired by the passionate love story of Jesus to guide your celebration of his birth.

As you allow these words to warm you this Christmas season, walk in the hope Joseph had when Gabriel visited him; rest in the peace Mary experienced when she was told she'd bear the Son of God; join her in shouting for joy in praise of the mighty Miracle Worker; and delight in God's furious, passionate love—a love so big and wide and deep that he sent his loving Son to suffer and die in your place.

Advent is a season to both celebrate Jesus' first coming and prepare for his second. I trust these encouraging words about the birth of God's Son will help you prepare him room this Christmas season—in your life, your home, your heart.

Now, let heaven and nature sing in celebration of our loving King!

WHAT IS THIS DEVOTIONAL, AND HOW SHOULD I USE IT?

"It's the most wonderful time of the year!"

The 1960s pop singer Andy Williams perfectly captures the emotion many of us feel during the Christmas season with his hit song of the same title. It really is the most wonderful, magical time of the year, isn't?

There's something about this season that makes people come alive, that draws out the inner child of even the "Scroogiest" of adults.

Perhaps it's how the snow transforms any landscape into an epic fairytale land.

Perhaps it's the smell of fresh-baked gingerbread out of the oven or a stew that's been simmering in the Crock-Pot all day. Or the taste of hot cocoa with a candy cane perched on the side.

Perhaps it's seeing the face of a child light up when she opens up that *one* present she's been dreaming about all winter long.

Of course as Christians, we know why it's so wonderful. The angels said it best: "Glory to God in the highest realms of heaven! For there is peace and a good hope given to the sons of men" (Luke 2:14).

Christmas time is the most wonderful time because a peace and a good hope have been gifted to humanity by the God of the universe! In fact, this peace and good hope were wrapped in the unlikeliest of ways: flesh and blood. Here is how the apostle John speaks about this gift:

> He was not born by the joining of human parents
> or from natural means, or by a man's desire,
> but he was born of God.
> And so the Living Expression
> became a man and lived among us!
> And we gazed upon the splendor of his glory,
> the glory of the One and Only
> who came from the Father overflowing
> with tender mercy and truth! (John 1:13–14)

This is the most wonderful time of the year because it is the time when God came to us by becoming one of us. And it is this gift, this coming, that we celebrate during this sacred season of Advent.

The term Advent may be unfamiliar to you. It is this time of anticipation and preparation that begins the Christian liturgical calendar and includes the four Sundays before Christmas. The name comes from the Latin word *adventus*, meaning "coming." During the Advent season, Christians prepare for the different "comings" of Christ—first as a baby born to take away the sins of the world, and second as the victorious King come again to put the world to rights.

If your particular Christian tradition celebrates Advent then you are already familiar with the Advent wreath and four candles, which help the church celebrate Christ's first coming: hope, peace, joy, and love. Each Sunday, a new candle is lit and a new theme is unpacked to help Christians reflect upon Christ's birth. It is this practice that inspired this Advent devotional using a faithful and fresh, reliable and relevant new translation of the Bible, *The Passion Translation.*

The Passion Translation is a groundbreaking attempt to reintroduce the passion and fire of the Bible to the English reader. It doesn't merely convey the original, literal meaning of words. It expresses God's passion for people and his world by translating the original, life-changing message of God's Word for modern readers.

God longs to have his Word expressed in every language in a way that would unlock the "passion" of his heart. Our goal is to trigger inside every English speaker an overwhelming response to the truth of the Bible, unfiltered by religious jargon. This is a heart-level translation, from the passion of

God's heart to the passion of your heart. And we've put this devotional together to help introduce you to it in a way that will bless your walk through the Christmas season.

This book is organized around the four weeks of Advent and its themes of hope, peace, joy, and love. Each week begins with a Psalm reading and section of the Christmas narrative from either Luke or Matthew, which coincides with the Advent readings of the liturgical calendar. You can choose to read the selection of Scripture at the beginning of the week on Monday, or do so at the start of each day. You'll find a short devotional along with Scripture passages from *The Passion Translation* for five days of the week, Monday through Friday, which are based on those Scripture readings. Christmas Eve (or Christmas Day, depending how you want to use it) has its own special reading and devotional.

We trust this version of God's Word will kindle in you a burning, passionate desire for him and his heart, while influencing the church for years to come. We also pray this Advent devotional will encourage and inspire your faith in the One who came to rescue us and the One who will come again to create us anew!

WEEK ONE

Hope

Week One

SCRIPTURE READINGS

PSALM 80:1–7, 17–19

[1] God-Enthroned, be revealed in splendor
as you ride upon the cherubim!
How perfectly you lead us, a people set free.
Loving shepherd of Israel—listen to our hearts' cry!
Shine forth from your throne of dazzling light.
[2] In the sight of Benjamin, Ephraim, and Manasseh,
stir up your mighty power in full display before
our eyes.
Break through and reveal yourself by coming to
our rescue.
[3] Revive us, O God! Let your beaming face shine
upon us
with the sunrise rays of glory;
then nothing will be able to stop us.

[4] O God, the mighty Commander of Angel Armies,
how much longer will you smolder in anger?
How much longer will you be disgusted with
your people
even when they pray?
[5] You have fed us with sorrow and grief
and made us drink our tears by the bowlful.
[6] You've made us a thorn in the side of all the
neighboring lands,
and now they just laugh at us with their mocking
scorn.
[7] Come back, come back, O God, and restore us!
You are the Commander of Angel Armies.
Let your beaming face shine upon us with the sunrise
rays of glory,
and then nothing will be able to stop us!
[17] Strengthen this Branch-Man, the Son of your love,
the Son of Man who dwells at your right hand.
[18] Then we will never turn back from you.
Revive us again, that we may trust in you.
[19] O God, the mighty Commander of Angel Armies,
come back and rescue us!
Let your beaming face shine upon us
with the sunrise rays of glory.
Then nothing will ever stop us again!

MATTHEW 1

From Abraham to Christ

[1] This is the scroll of the lineage and birth of Jesus, the Anointed One, the son of David and descendant of Abraham.

[2] Abraham had a son named Isaac, who had a son named Jacob, who had a son named Judah (he and his brothers became the tribes of Israel).

[3] Judah and Tamar had twin sons, Perez and Zerah. Perez had a son named Hezron, who had a son named Ram, [4] who had a son named Amminadab, who had a son named Nashon, [5] who had a son named Salmon, who, along with Rahab, had a son named Boaz. Boaz and Ruth had a son named Obed, who was the father of Jesse, [6] and Jesse had a son named David, who became the king.

[7] Then David and Bathsheba had a son named Solomon, who had a son named Rehoboam, who had a son named Abijah, who had a son named Asa, [8] who had a son named Jehoshaphat, who had a son named Joram, who had a son named Uzziah, [9] who had a son named Jotham, who had a son named Ahaz, who had a son named Hezekiah, [10] who had a son named Manasseh, who had a son named Amos, who had a son named Josiah, [11] who was the father of Jeconiah.

It was during the days of Jeconiah and his brothers that Israel was taken captive and deported to Babylon. [12] About the time of their captivity in Babylon, Jeconiah had a son named

Shealtiel, who had a son named Zerubbabel, [13] who had a son named Abiud, who had a son named Eliakim, [14] who had a son named Azor, who had a son named Zadok, who had a son named Achim, who had a son named Eliud, [15] who had a son named Eleazar, who had a son named Matthan, who had a son named Jacob, [16] who was the father of Joseph, the husband of Mary the mother of Jesus, who is called "the Anointed One."

[17] So from Abraham to David were fourteen generations, and from David to the Babylonian captivity, fourteen generation, and from the Babylonian captivity to Christ, fourteen generations.

An Angel Comes to Joseph

[18] This was how Jesus, God's Anointed One, was born.

His mother, Mary, had promised Joseph to be his wife, but while she was still a virgin she became pregnant through the power of the Holy Spirit. [19] Her fiancé, Joseph, was a righteous man full of integrity and he didn't want to disgrace her, but when he learned of her pregnancy he secretly planned to break the engagement. [20] While he was still debating with himself about what to do, he fell asleep and had a supernatural dream. An angel from the Lord appeared to him in clear light and said, "Joseph, descendant of David, don't hesitate to take Mary into your home as your wife, because the power of the Holy Spirit has conceived a child in her womb. [21] She will give birth to a son and you are to name him 'Savior,' for he is destined to give his life to save his people from their sins."

[22] This happened so that what the Lord spoke through his prophet would come true:

[23] Listen! A virgin will be pregnant,
she will give birth to a Son,
and he will be known as "Emmanuel,"
which means in Hebrew,
"God became one of us."

[24] When Joseph awoke from his dream, he did all that the angel of the Lord instructed him to do. He took Mary to be his wife, [25] but they refrained from having sex until she gave birth to her son, whom they named "Jesus."

Day 1

NOTHING WILL BE ABLE TO STOP US!

(Psalm 80:1–7)

Throughout history—even during Christmastime—the church of Jesus Christ has cried out to God during times of persecution, decline, and internal strife.

Under the Roman Emperor Nero, Christians suffered immense persecution—being burned at the stake to light his courtyards, crucified on crosses lining Roman highways, and murdered in the Colosseum to the delight of Roman citizens. They cried out, "Why, Lord?"

During the second through fifth centuries, the early church experienced intense internal strife because of false teachers bent on warping the message of Christ and his church. Leaders like Irenaeus, Athanasius, and Augustine all asked, "Why, God?"

During the Middle Ages, Muslim hordes butchered and ransacked Christian towns, churches, and holy sites throughout Northern Africa, the Middle East, and much of Europe. And the collective Body of Christ wondered, "Why?"

Then, during the Great Awakenings in the eighteenth and nineteenth centuries of America, the likes of Jonathan Edwards, George Whitfield, and D.L. Moody cried out to God to revive the churches and her members, wondering why the "city on a hill" of religious freedom known as America had become watered down.

More recently, Western churches are mourning their demise and praying for a restoration of the great times of the past. The world-wide church is asking the question the people of God have asked for millennium: "Why, Lord?"

The same was true of Israel's story too, which Psalm 80 represents. This song of lament was a prayer members of tribes of Judah offered up to God. They were in decline, they were in trouble, they had been rejected by God because of rebellion.

Sounds familiar, doesn't it?

And so the people of God got on their knees and sang or said this psalm as a prayer, asking the "Loving Shepherd of Israel [to] listen to our hearts' cry!"

They wanted him to "stir up your mighty power" and "break through and reveal yourself by coming to our rescue."

They longed for God to "revive us," to "let your beaming face shine upon us with the sunrise rays of glory."

Because if he did, "Then nothing will be able to stop us."

This same song and prayer was probably on the lips of Jews living in Palestine under Roman occupation two thousand years ago too.

They were in decline, in trouble, they hadn't heard from God in nearly four centuries, and they were waiting for the Anointed One—the "Branch-Man, the Son of your love, the Son of Man who dwells at your right hand" (Ps. 80:17).

God promised this One would come to save them, rescue them, and put them back together again.

And guess what? He did!

The Branch-Man did come to revive and rescue, but not just Israel. For as Luke wrote, "The Son of Man has come to seek out and to give life to those who are lost" (Luke 19:10). All the lost, not just lost Israel.

As the church looks around us this Christmas season, we may feel like Israel felt: we're in decline, we're in trouble, our nation needs restoration. While we could pray this prayer along with Israel, the truth is God fulfilled their hearts' cry—and ours!

The promised Branch-Man came in full glory and power to reveal God, rescue, revive, and restore us.

And because he did, nothing can ever stop us—not even

the power of death will be able to overpower the church (Matt. 16:18).

Advent Prayer of Hope

Commander of Angel-Armies, while things may seem hopeless for your people, remind us this Christmas season that your Branch-Man, the Son of your love and the One who dwells at your right hand, has come in full glory and power to reveal, rescue, revive, and restore!

Day 2

EVERY GREAT STORY HAS A GREAT BEGINNING

(Matthew 1:1–17)

Think about your favorite stories and how they begin.

For Charles Dickens, "It was the best of times, it was the worst of times." "Once there were four children whose names were Peter, Susan, Edmund, and Lucy," opens *The Lion, the Witch and the Wardrobe.* A recent favorite opener is probably this one: "Mr. and Mrs. Dursley, of number four, Privet Drive, were proud to say that they were perfectly normal, thank you very much"—which introduced a generation to Harry Potter.

Every great story has a great beginning. The story of Jesus is no different, yet most of us miss its significance. Check out its first line:

"This is the scroll of the lineage and birth of Jesus, the Anointed One, the son of David and descendant of Abraham."

There are two things to notice here. The first is that the gospel of Matthew is a "scroll of the lineage and birth of Jesus, the Anointed One." Another way of translating this is "the book of the origin of Jesus Christ." *Lineage* and *origin* are connected to the Greek word *geneseos*, which is where we get *Genesis*.

Matthew wants us to do a Genesis double take. He wants us to remember the original creation and what happened shortly thereafter—mainly our rebellion against our Creator—but then look to the *re*-creation happening in Jesus. In other words, the broken, busted original creation is being re-created anew through Jesus, the Anointed One!

What's remarkable about this story and its beginning is that it doesn't begin here at all but, well, back at the beginning—which Matthew helps us remember by tracing Jesus' story back to David and through to Abraham.

After humanity ruined creation by rebelling against God, he got to work to make things right again by choosing a man named Abraham to be the vessel through which the Lord would bless all peoples on earth. He formed a relationship with Abraham and his offspring, which he renewed with David along with a promise of an heir who would establish his reign and God's promises forever.

Matthew's genealogy presents the legal claim of Jesus to

be King through the lineage of David from Joseph all the way back to the promises given to Abraham.

The beginning of Jesus' story reminds us that God made good on his plan and promise to rescue this world and put it back together again, which should give us hope. Because no matter how dark things look and tough things get, God has a plan. He also has a number of promises, which he will fulfill for you—just like he did for his own Son.

Advent Prayer of Hope

God, this Christmas season I am thankful that you had a plan from the beginning to rescue and re-create the world. Remind me of this when things look dark and things get tough. Amen.

Day 3

WHAT'S IN THE NAME OF JESUS?

(Matthew 1:20–21)

"What's in a name?" William Shakespeare wrote in his famous play, *Romeo and Juliet*. "That which we call a rose by any other name would smell as sweet."

While Shakespeare implied that the name of things doesn't affect what they really are, that was not the case in Jesus' day, especially when it came to people's names.

Think back to the story of Jacob and Esau. Genesis 25 says when the first boy was born he was like a hairy garment, so he was named Esau, which means "hairy." When the second boy was born he was grasping the heel of his brother, so he was named Jacob, which means "he grasps the heel." As the story unfolds, we find out just how meaningful this name of Jacob's really is.

The same was true for Isaac, whose name means "laughter," inspired by the fact Abraham laughed when God told him he would give Isaac to him and his wife.

Now think about the name *Jesus*. Joseph was commanded by the angel of the Lord to specifically name his Son, Jesus. Why? Why *this* name?

Do you know what Jesus' name means? The full depth and majesty of his name isn't grasped initially, because the version we know is in its Greek form, *Iesous*. Its Hebrew form, however, helps us more fully understand the significance of Jesus' name—and, more importantly, who he was and what he came to do.

The Hebrew version of Jesus is *Yeshua* (or *Y'hoshua*), which means "Yahweh is Salvation, Restoration, and Deliverance" or "God saves, restores, and delivers."

Of course, that is exactly what God did by sending his Son, Yeshua, to be born of the Virgin Mary: He came to save us, to deliver us, to rescue and restore us!

Though Shakespeare believed names were not important, we know otherwise. The one we call Jesus, by any other name, would not be as precious to us because he did what we could not do ourselves.

He saved, restored, and delivered us because he *is* salvation, restoration, and deliverance.

And that should give us a tremendous amount of hope this Advent! Because as Paul wrote in Ephesians:

> Even when we were dead and doomed in our many sins, he united us into the very life of Christ and saved us by his wonderful grace! He raised us up with Christ the exalted One, and we ascended with him into the glorious perfection and authority of the heavenly realm, for we are now co-seated[a] as one with Christ! (Eph. 2:5–6)

Advent Prayer of Hope

Jesus, Name above all names, this Christmas season I praise you for your name because of what it means for me and the whole entire world: salvation, restoration, deliverance, and ultimately hope. Amen.

Day 4

THE GOD WHO LIVED YOUR LIFE

(Matthew 1:23)

Do you ever wonder if God understands your life? Whether he *really* understands what it means to be human and deal with all the stuff we have to deal with—the stress and worry, the health scares and difficult teenagers, the bills and demanding bosses?

Amazingly he does! We don't serve a distant and removed God, like the Romans and the Greeks did. No we serve a God who, in the words of the angel who visited Joseph, "became one of us!"

As a good Jew, along with all of his people, Joseph would have been waiting for the Anointed One God promised to send to save his people. What Joseph—or his people for that matter—would not have expected was that God, through the power of the Holy Spirit, would conceive a child in his fiancée's womb and "be known as 'Emmanuel,' which means 'God became one of us'" (Luke 1:21, 23).

Look at how various people throughout the New Testament described this monumental Emmanuel-event:

John says in his Gospel that "the Living Expression [Jesus Christ] became a man and lived among us! And we gazed upon the splendor of his glory, the glory of the One and Only, who came from the Father overflowing with tender mercy and truth" (1:14).

The writer of Hebrews wrote, "Since all his 'children' have flesh and blood, so Jesus became human to fully identify with us. He did this, so that he could experience death and annihilate the effects of the intimidating accuser who holds against us the power of death" (2:14).

He doesn't stop there, though; he goes on: "For we have a magnificent King-Priest, Jesus Christ, the Son of God, who rose into the heavenly realm for us, and now sympathizes with us in our frailty. He understands humanity, for as a Man, our magnificent King-Priest was tempted in every way just as we are, and conquered sin. So now we come freely and boldly to where love is enthroned, to receive mercy's kiss and discover the grace we urgently need to strengthen us in our time of weakness" (4:14–16).

Think about this: The God of the universe "sympathizes with us in our frailty," he "understands humanity." How? Because he "became a man and lived among us," as John says! He "became human to fully identify with us!"

God lived this life, which means he understands your life—all of your frailty and pain, your baggage and brokenness.

He understands humiliation because *he* was humiliated on the cross. He understands rejection because *he* was rejected. He understands sorrow because *he* was a man of sorrows.

Do you ever wonder if God understands your life? Well, wonder no more! Because the beauty and majesty of the Christmas season is that Mary gave birth to Emmanuel, to the God who became one of us.

May this truth give us all hope as we celebrate the first coming of the God-with-us God!

Advent Prayer of Hope

God, I thank you for becoming one of us and experiencing all that life has to offer. May it give me strength for today and bright hope for tomorrow knowing that you understand my life because you lived my life. Amen.

Day 5

WHAT DO YOU DO WHEN LIFE DOESN'T TURN OUT THE WAY YOU THOUGHT IT WOULD?

(Matthew 1:24–25)

What do you do when life doesn't turn out the way you thought that it would?

How do you respond when you lose your job in a corporate merger? Or when you get that phone call with the results of that medical test? How about when a relationship falls apart?

Consider the life of Joseph, husband to Mary and stepfather to Jesus.

One day things were great—engaged to be married, a successful carpenter, a man of integrity with a good name for himself, an upstanding Jewish young man.

The next day, however, his life takes an unexpected turn when he learns his wife-to-be is pregnant.

In Joseph's day that meant instant shame and finger-pointing. He would have been pressured to break the engagement and abandon Mary, even put her on trial as an adulteress and make sure she was punished as a law-breaker.

The next day things change, yet again, because when he was still deciding what to do with his fiancée, the angel of Lord appeared to him in a supernatural dream with a world-rocking message:

> "Joseph, descendant of David, don't hesitate to take Mary into your home as your wife, because the power of the Holy Spirit has conceived a child in her womb. She will give birth to a son and you are to name him 'Savior,' for he is destined to give his life to save his people from their sins." (Matt. 1:20–21)

What would you do? Shrug the experience off as a hallucination? Or take it seriously?

What did Joseph do? Check it out:

"When Joseph awoke from his dream, he did all that the angel of the Lord instructed him to do. He took Mary to be his wife, but they refrained from having sex until she gave birth to her son, whom they named, 'Jesus'" (Matt. 1:24–25).

So what did Joseph do when his life didn't turn out the way he thought it would?

He obeyed.

He might not have understood what was going on—what man would have understood the idea of God conceiving his Son supernaturally through his wife-to-be? He was probably scared at what it meant for him and his life. But instead of running, instead of turning on God, instead of pointing fingers at him turning his life on end, Joseph obeyed. In hope, he trusted in the promises God spoke over him.

During Advent we often forget the man who stood in the shadows of his fiancée and stepson. Yet Joseph's story is a hope-filled one. May we remember the hope-filled example Joseph provides us in faithfulness and obedience to God, especially in those moments when life doesn't turn out the way we thought that it would.

Advent Prayer of Hope

Heavenly Father, I thank you for the story of Joseph and for his example of obedience. May I follow his hope-filled example by trusting in the promises you have for my life—no matter how much life doesn't turn out the way I thought that it would. Amen.

Week Two

Peace

SCRIPTURE READINGS

PSALM 85:1–2, 8–13

[1] Lord, your love has poured out
so many amazing blessings on our land!
You've restored Jacob's destiny from captivity.
[2] You've forgiven our many sins and covered
every one of them in your love.

Pause in his presence

[8] Now I'll listen carefully for your voice
and wait to hear whatever you say.
Let me hear your promise of peace—
the message every one of your godly lovers longs to hear.
Don't let us in our ignorance turn back from following you.
[9] For I know your power and presence shines on all
your lovers.

Your glory always hovers over all who bow low before you.
[10] Your mercy and your truth have married each other.
Your righteousness and peace have kissed.
[11] Flowers of your faithfulness are blooming on the earth.
Righteousness shines down from the sky.
[12] Yes, the Lord keeps raining down blessing after blessing,
and prosperity will drench the land with a bountiful harvest.
[13] For deliverance and peace are his forerunners,
preparing a path for his steps.

LUKE 1:5–38

The Birth of the Prophet John

[5] During the reign of King Herod the Great over Judea, there was a Jewish priest named Zechariah who served in the temple as part of the priestly order of Abijah. His wife, Elizabeth, was also from a family of priests, being a direct descendant of Aaron. [6] They were both lovers of God, living virtuously and following the commandments of the Lord fully. [7] But they were childless since Elizabeth was barren, and now they both were quite old.

[8–9] One day, while Zechariah's priestly order was on duty and he was serving as priest, it happened by the casting of lots (according to the custom of the priesthood) that the honor fell upon Zechariah to enter into the Holy Place and burn incense before the Lord. [10] A large crowd of worshipers had gathered to pray outside the temple at the hour when incense was being offered. [11] All at once an angel of the Lord appeared to him, standing just to the right of the altar of incense.

[12] Zechariah was startled and overwhelmed with fear. [13] But the angel reassured him, saying, "Don't be afraid, Zechariah! God is showing grace to you. For I have come to tell you that your prayer for a child has been answered. Your wife, Elizabeth, will bear you a son and you are to name him John. [14] His birth will bring you much joy and gladness. Many will rejoice because of him. [15] He will be one of the great ones in the sight of God. He will drink no wine or strong drink, but he will be filled with the Holy Spirit even while still in his mother's womb. [16] And he will persuade many in Israel to convert and turn back to the Lord their God. [17] He will go before the Lord as a forerunner, with the same power and anointing as Elijah the prophet. He will be instrumental in turning the hearts of the fathers in tenderness back to their children and the hearts of the disobedient back to the wisdom of their righteous fathers. And he will prepare a united people who are ready for the Lord's appearing."

[18] Zechariah asked the angel, "How do you expect me to believe this? I'm an old man and my wife is too old to give me a child. What sign can you give me to prove this will happen?"

[19] Then the angel said, "I am Gabriel. I stand beside God

himself. He has sent me to announce to you this good news. [20] But now, since you did not believe my words, you will be stricken silent and unable to speak until the day my words have been fulfilled at their appointed time and a child is born to you. That will be your sign!"

[21] Meanwhile, the crowds outside kept expecting him to come out. They were amazed over Zechariah's delay, wondering what could have happened inside the sanctuary. [22] When he finally did come out, he tried to talk, but he couldn't speak a word, and they realized from his gestures that he had seen a vision while in the Holy Place. [23] He remained mute as he finished his days of priestly ministry in the temple and then went back to his own home. [24] Soon afterward his wife, Elizabeth, became pregnant and went into seclusion for the next five months. [25] She said with joy, "See how kind it is of God to gaze upon me and take away the disgrace of my barrenness!"

Angelic Prophecy of Jesus' Birth

[26-27] During the sixth month of Elizabeth's pregnancy, the angel Gabriel was sent from God's presence to an unmarried girl named Mary, living in Nazareth, a village in Galilee. She was engaged to a man named Joseph, a true descendant of King David. [28] Gabriel appeared to her and said, "Grace to you, young woman, for the Lord is with you and so you are anointed with great favor."

[29] Mary was deeply troubled over the words of the angel and bewildered over what this may mean for her. [30] But the

angel reassured her, saying, "Do not yield to your fear, Mary, for the Lord has found delight in you and has chosen to surprise you with a wonderful gift. [31] You will become pregnant with a baby boy, and you are to name him Jesus. [32] He will be supreme and will be known as the Son of the Highest. And the Lord God will enthrone him as King on his ancestor David's throne. [33] He will reign as King of Israel forever, and his reign will have no limit."

[34] Mary said, "But how could this happen? I am still a virgin!"

[35] Gabriel answered, "The Spirit of Holiness will fall upon you and almighty God will spread his shadow of power over you in a cloud of glory! This is why the child born to you will be holy, and he will be called the Son of God. [36] What's more, your aged aunt, Elizabeth, has also become pregnant with a son. The 'barren one' is now in her sixth month. [37] Not one promise from God is empty of power, for nothing is impossible with God!"

[38] Then Mary responded, saying, "This is amazing! I will be a mother for the Lord! As his servant, I accept whatever he has for me. May everything you have told me come to pass." And the angel left her.

Day 1

THE PROMISE OF THE LORD'S PEACE— IN A PIECE OF CANDY

(Psalm 85:1–2, 8–13)

Do you know the story of the candy cane?

Well, there's an old legend about a nice old candy maker in Indiana. He loved to make candy, especially for little boys and girls.

One Christmas he decided to make a special kind of candy that would tell a special story, the story of Jesus.

The nice old candy maker from Indiana took a stick of pure white, hard candy. The color white reminds us that he never sinned.

If you've ever eaten a candy cane, you know how hard it is,

right? Like a rock. Mr. Candy Maker made it hard—to remind us that Jesus is our shelter—like a rocky cave.

And what letter does it look like? Yes a J! Which not only represents the name Jesus, but also the staff of the "Good Shepherd." A shepherd picks up sheep with the rounded end then fights off wild animals with the other. Jesus helps us and keeps us safe.

Finally the candy maker put three reds stripes around it to remind us of the pain Jesus went through on the cross for our sins, all so that we can be with God forever and have a life of peace.

So that's the story of the candy cane. It tells us of Jesus and his great love for each of us. It also tells us of the peace we can have in life because of what he did.

Peace. What an interesting word. Peace is a hard thing to come by—peace for life, relationships, our health, our bank accounts, our jobs, our memories, our souls.

If you look in a thesaurus you'll see the opposite words for peace are *agitation* and *distress*. A pretty good way to talk about life most of the time. And yet, the psalmist reminds us of a promised peace, a message every one of God's godly lovers longs to hear.

Psalm 85 begins by remembering the peace Yahweh brought his people in the past: "[He] restored Jacob's destiny from captivity," and he forgave their "many sins and covered every one of them in [his] love."

Next he listens for what Yahweh has to say. And what he has to say is this: the promise of peace. God's power and presence is shining, his glory hovers over his people. Mercy and truth, righteousness and peace are kissing. Faithfulness is blooming, righteousness is shining. The Lord will give good things because "deliverance and peace are his forerunners preparing a path for his steps."

In other words: peace and restoration are coming!

From the very beginning of our human story God promised to do something about all of the agitation and distress in our world. He promised to restore the peace.

And he did. He sent the Prince of Peace to come and do what we can't do for ourselves. Jesus brings true, lasting peace. Jesus' story announces in big, bright, bold colors the kind of peace that all of us are desperately searching for—which is offered to all people.

As the angel of the Lord said that first Christmas Eve:

> "Glory to God in the highest realms of heaven!
> For there is peace and a good hope given to the sons of men." (Luke 2:14)

May we know the promises of that peace deep down this Christmas season.

Advent Prayer of Peace

Father God, I thank you for sending us your promised peace by sending us your Son. May what the Prince of Peace accomplished in his life and death guard my heart and mind from the agitation and distress of the world this Advent season. Amen.

Day 2

WHETHER BAD NEWS OR TOO-GOOD-TO-BE-TRUE NEWS, GOD REALLY CAN BE TRUSTED!

(Luke 1:5–24)

How many times have we heard Gabriel's command before, "Don't be afraid"? In fact, it's one of the most frequent commands in the Bible.

Why is that?

Perhaps it's because God knows us all too well: We humans are so prone to fear! And when we fear, it leads to a lack of peace, which often leads to unbelief. Whether bad news or too-good-to-be-true news, it's in those moments we feel the least at peace and we often have the least faith.

Think about it. You receive disappointing news, and your world is disrupted. Or you receive unbelievable news, and you still feel your world has been turned upside down. Like Zechariah's world.

Here was Zechariah, a faithful servant of Yahweh faithfully serving in the temple when his world was disrupted and turned upside down thanks to Gabriel's announcement.

"God is showing grace to you," he proclaims. "For I have come to tell you that your prayer for a child has been answered. Your wife, Elizabeth, will bear you a son, and you are to name him John" (1:13).

Now while we might fear such news, this is the good kind of disruption and world-turning news many of us would want to hear! And yet how does Zechariah respond?

"How do you expect me to believe this? I'm an old man, and my wife is too old to give me a child. What sign can you give me to prove this will happen?" (1:18)

Perhaps this unbelief was born out of his fear from verse 12, fear that his prayers and deepest hopes might not actually come true after all, fear for what it might mean for him and his wife if they did believe.

Regardless, it's obvious he doesn't have peace about the news, which seems to fuel his unbelief. Instead of joy and peace, hope, and faith—which you'd expect from a priest in God's holy temple—Zechariah expresses agitation, distress, and doubt—the exact opposite of peace and faith.

How does Gabriel respond?

"Since you did not believe my words, you will be stricken silent and unable to speak until the day my words have been fulfilled at their appointed time and a child is born to you. That will be your sign!" (1:20)

Some sign! Zechariah's world is about to be disrupted even more for his unbelief.

Notice how he demands to *know*, while Gabriel emphasizes *belief*. When life crashes or we receive a confusing, too-good-to-be-true calling on our lives, often we demand to *know*—why it happened or how it will happen and whether or not it will all work out in the end. And rather than resting in the peace of God because we hope in him and his promises, all we feel is agitation and disruption.

Next week you'll experience another story about unexpected news—perhaps as, or even more, unbelievable! Yet the reaction is totally different. While Zechariah is a negative example of peace and faith, Mary shows us how it looks to truly have faith in the Prince of Peace.

This Christmas, may we learn from Zechariah's example of agitation and disruption, his example of doubt and unbelief. Unlike Zechariah, may we learn to believe God's words to us for the plan he has for our lives—whether that news is bad news or too-good-to-be-true news. Because if there's anything Zechariah's story teaches us it's that God really can be trusted—which should bring us great peace!

Advent Prayer of Peace

Heavenly Father, who knows exactly what I need, help me trust you when you announce a word of news over my life—whether bad news or too-good-to-be-true news. May I have faith in your Word, and may that Word give me peace.

Day 3

ARE YOU A FORERUNNER OF THE PRINCE OF PEACE?

(Luke 1:14–17)

Do you know what a *forerunner* is? Are you one?

Dictionary.com says a forerunner is "a person or thing coming in advance to herald the arrival of someone or something."

Two thousand years ago, an angel of the Lord announced to a very old man, Zechariah, that his yet-unborn-child would "go before the Lord as a *forerunner*"—as a person coming in advance to announce the arrival of someone else.

That someone else was Jesus!

When Zechariah's son, John, began his ministry, the apostle John records that he described it in this way: "I am fulfilling Isaiah's prophecy: 'I am an urgent, thundering voice shouting in the desert—clear the way and prepare your hearts for the coming of the Lord Yahweh!'"

John made it clear he was not the Anointed One come to save the world; he was his forerunner, the one who came to clear the way and prepare people's hearts for his coming. And when the Lord did come, John got out of the way and turned all eyes on Jesus: "Look! There he is—God's Lamb! He will take away the sins of the world!" (John 1:29).

For years John carried with him the message about what Jesus would do: rescue the world and put it back together again by taking away our sins. Isaiah says such people who carry good news, proclaim peace, bear good tidings, and preach salvation from mountain to mountain have "beautiful feet."

John's feet were beautiful because he was a forerunner—running before the Prince of Peace to announce his coming peace. Are yours as beautiful? Are you a forerunner of the Lord, like John?

Do you know the Bible describes one other person as a forerunner? Who do you think it was? Yes, Jesus Christ himself! Read how the author of Hebrews describes our Lord:

> "We have this certain hope like a strong, unbreakable anchor holding our souls to God himself. Our anchor of hope is fastened to the mercy seat which

> sits in the heavenly realm beyond the sacred threshold, and where Jesus, our *forerunner*, has gone in before us. He is now and forever our royal Priest like Melchizedek." (Heb. 6:19–20)

Jesus is our forerunner because "he has entered once and forever into the Holiest Sanctuary of All, not with the blood of animal sacrifices, but the sacred blood of his own sacrifice. And he alone has made our salvation secure forever" (Heb. 9:12).

Because of Jesus' life, death, and resurrection we have been declared not guilty through our faith in him—which has brought us peace with God (Rom. 5:1). Because he was pierced for our rebellion and crushed for our sins, we have peace and we've been healed (Isa. 53:5).

This message of peace and healing is the message John carried with him into his world. We are invited to follow his lead by carrying that same message of peace and healing with us as well.

This Christmas, may you shout from the rooftops or the mountains that the Savior of the world has been born. May you carry to the people in your life the same peace you've experienced by announcing the arrival of the Prince of Peace—so that your feet are declared as beautiful as John's!

Advent Prayer of Peace

Jesus, this Advent I want to do what John did: announce the arrival of your peace, healing, forgiveness, and rescue! May you give me the courage to follow his example as your forerunner. Amen.

Day 4

HOW COULD THIS HAPPEN?

(Luke 1:26–38)

Sometimes there are those moments in life when everything just *shifts*.

You're driving along, and all of a sudden brake lights—and then your front end ends up in the back end of the car in front of you. *Life shift.*

Your teenage daughter sits you down and says she got a blue plus sign on the white stick she bought at the local pharmacy; she's pregnant. *Life shift.*

Your aging parent gets the results you were dreading—Alzheimer's, and the next twenty years you'll be caring for her. *Life shift.*

And in each scenario you're left saying, "How could this happen?"

Now imagine you're minding your own business, and

an angel of the Lord appears to you and says, "The Lord has found delight in you and has chosen to surprise you with a wonderful gift. You will become pregnant with a baby boy, and you are to name him Jesus."

Major *life shift*! Of course that's exactly what happened to Mary.

Ever wonder what was going through her mind? Confusion? Nervousness? Excitement? Fear?

Probably lots of the former and lots of the latter because as she said, "But how could this happen? I'm still a virgin!"

Mary was most likely thirteen years old—at the most sixteen. Not twenty or thirty like she's often portrayed in movies and Christmas pageants. Thirteen.

She was also engaged—which in her world meant she and Joseph were legally married, except for the sexual relations part, which came later. And now she was pregnant, which had major social consequences for Mary and Joseph *and* Jesus. Since Mary and Joseph were legally married, any sexual relations outside that relationship would have been considered adultery—she would have been labeled a *sotah*, a suspected adulteress.

Immediately after hearing these words from the angel that she was pregnant she would have connected her pregnancy to being a *sotah*—and everything that came with it. The humiliation, the shame from a public trial to determine her guilt. She would have wondered how Joseph would respond to the news, being that he was a good Torah-observing Jew. Would he go through with the trial? Divorce her as the Law required? Leave her stranded and financially ruined?

She probably feared for her unborn child too, for when he grew up. Fear for the taunts and accusations of being a *mamzar*—an illegitimate child—and everything that label carried with it.

And yet, how did Mary respond?

Let's be honest, if it was any one of us we might have gotten angry at this life shift. We for sure would have feared its consequences.

Not Mary. Instead she replied, "This is amazing! I will be a mother for the Lord! As his servant, I accept whatever he has for me. May everything you have told me come to pass."

Instead of yielding to her fears because of her shifted circumstances, she was at peace with them. And that peace gave her the courage to obey, to accept whatever it was the Lord had for her.

May Mary's example of peace compel us this Christmas season to accept whatever life-shift moments come our way in the coming year. And may we look to her Son, the Prince of Peace, to be *our* peace.

Advent Prayer of Peace

*Lord Jesus Christ, my Prince of Peace, I come to you to tell you every detail of my life, so that "God's wonderful peace that transcends human understanding, will make the answers known to [me] through Jesus Christ" (Phil. 4:7). *Spend a moment pouring out the details of your life.*

Day 5

A TALE OF TWO REACTIONS

(Luke 1:5–38)

When you are brought unexpected news, how do you typically react? Do you start freaking out or take it in stride? Fear or have faith it will all work out? Do you get agitated and distressed or react with calm and peace?

This week has been a lesson in two reactions to unexpected, distressing news. Read through our Advent passage again and notice the two very different responses to a very similar message received from the angel Gabriel.

Both Zechariah and Mary were told they would have a child. And both of them shouldn't have been able to, given their circumstances. Yet how do they respond?

Remember how Zechariah responds? Disbelief. He had no

peace about this announcement, given he was an old man and his wife was too old to give him a child.

Then what happened? The angel disrupted his life even more by taking away his speech—all because of his disbelief and lack of peace.

What about Mary? A few days ago you read about and meditated upon Mary's response. Instead of disbelieving as Zechariah did, Mary had complete peace with her life shift. And then she responded in faith and believed out of that peace.

What a totally different reaction! It reflects what the story itself says when the angel visits Mary with the news of her pregnancy: "I accept whatever he has for me. May everything you have told me come to pass" (Luke 1:38).

In Mary's song that follows she predicted that "Everyone will know that I have been favored and blessed" (Luke 1:48). Teenage Mary could never have understood what that declaration would mean—both for the world *and* for her.

She had peace with God's word to her, trusted in his hopeful plan for her life, and responded out of that peace and hope by inviting God to literally be born in her.

Do you share Mary's peace and trust and invitation? Or do you distress and disbelieve in fear, like Zechariah?

The greatest peace anyone can find is to follow in the steps of Mary and find their peace and hope in the God who saves.

Advent Prayer of Peace

Lord, I recognize when life shifts I can have two responses: either fear or faith. May I follow Mary's lead by trusting in your Word and hoping in your plan—knowing that her way is the way of true and lasting peace.

WEEK THREE

Week Three

SCRIPTURE READINGS

PSALM 126

[1] It was like a dream come true
when you freed us from our bondage and brought us
back to Zion!
[2] We laughed and laughed and overflowed with
gladness.
We were left shouting for joy and singing your praise.
All the nations saw it and joined in, saying,
"The Lord has done great miracles for them!"
[3] Yes, he did mighty miracles and we are overjoyed!
[4] Now, Lord, do it again! Restore us to our
former glory!
May streams of your refreshing flow over us
until our dry hearts are drenched again.
[5] Those who sow their tears as seeds

will reap a harvest with joyful shouts of glee.
[6] They may weep as they go out carrying their seed
to sow,
but they will return with joyful laughter and shouting
with gladness
as they bring back armloads of blessing and a harvest
overflowing!

LUKE 1:46–55

Mary's Prophetic Song

[46] And Mary sang this song:
"My soul is ecstatic, overflowing with praises to God!
[47] My spirit bursts with joy over my life-giving God!
[48] For he set his tender gaze upon me, his lowly
servant girl.
And from here on, everyone will know
that I have been favored and blessed.
[49] The Mighty One has worked a mighty miracle
for me;
holy is his name!
[50] Mercy kisses all his godly lovers,
from one generation to the next.
[51] Mighty power flows from him
to scatter all those who walk in pride.
[52] Powerful princes he tears from their thrones
and he lifts up the lowly to take their place.
[53] Those who hunger for him will always be filled,

but the smug and self-satisfied he will send away
empty.
[54] Because he can never forget to show mercy,
he has helped his chosen servant, Israel,
[55] Keeping his promises to Abraham
and to his descendants forever."

Day 1

LORD, DO IT AGAIN!

(Psalm 126)

Have you faced a tough situation that caused you to shout, "Not again!"?

Maybe you got a flat tire after you just replaced another one after a blowout. Or you got a chest cold after recovering from the flu. Perhaps it was more serious: your furnace gave out the day after you were laid off from work; your cancer returned after having been "free and clear" for years; your child was caught drinking and driving, for the second time.

Israel faced their own "Not again!" situation.

Many of us know the story of the Exodus, when they were slaves in Egypt under an oppressive dictator. Then one day the Lord heard their cries and delivered them from Egypt, through the Red Sea, and eventually brought them safely to the Promised Land.

Fast forward tens of generations later. The Israelites found themselves in the same situation: slaves of the oppressive empire of Babylon. Like before, the people cried out, "Not again!" And like before, the Lord delivered them and brought them back to their land.

But the story doesn't end there. Because they returned only to find their nation completely ruined. Homes were smashed, crops were left to rot, families were torn apart.

When they were released from captivity they "laughed and laughed," the poet writes in Psalm 126. They "overflowed with gladness." Now it's a different story. Now their hearts are dry, they are sowing tears like seeds.

Israel needed the Lord to do for them what he did before in Egypt and then again in Babylon. Following their "Not again!" cry was another one: "Lord, do it again!"

During the time when Jesus was born, more than likely Jews sang or prayed this very psalm while they were under Roman occupation. Yet again, their land was in ruins, overrun by pagan Rome. So they sang "Lord, do it again!"

And he did, but in a way they didn't expect.

While they were looking for a king to do battle with Rome, the Lord had something else in mind. Instead of sending an anointed warrior king, he sent an anointed Shepherd King to quench thirsty souls, wipe away people's tears, return their laughter and joy, and bring a harvest of overflowing blessing by healing the sick, restoring sight to the blind, and setting free those held captive by sin and shame.

Perhaps you find yourself in a situation this Christmas season where you're shouting, "Lord, not again!" Do what Israel did: boldly, confidently come before God's throne of grace asking, "Lord, *do it* again!"

Remember, two thousand years ago God brought deliverance for his people and for us when he sent his anointed shepherd king to rescue us from our sins and restore us to our former glory. He will do it again—and again!—in any number of ways, and on the other side we will experience what Israel experienced:

We will "return with joyful laughter, and shouting with gladness as [we] bring back armloads of blessing, and a harvest overflowing!"

Advent Prayer of Joy

Lord, I need you to do it again! Do for me this season what you did for Israel and for the world when you sent your Son: rescue me and restore me to for my former glory, so that I may return with joyful laughter. Amen.

Day 2

MARY'S HEAD-TURNING RESPONSE TO HER REMARKABLE NEWS

(Luke 1:46–55)

If you've ever been blessed to have a child, or have known others who have been pregnant, you know it's a time that's filled with lots of different emotions.

For those who have been trying, there is a sense of overwhelming joy for the little peanut that's on his or her way. The first ultrasound only increases that feeling of elation. But as the due date approaches, the apprehension over the changes that are coming and over the inadequacies can be pretty overwhelming.

For those who haven't been trying to have a baby, however, it's an entirely different situation. Anger and fear may rule the other side of the pregnancy test. Anger that it happened and how it will disrupt life, fear for what others will think and how they'll pay for it.

How do you suppose Mary felt when she found out she was pregnant? Probably a mixture of confusion, nervousness, excitement, and fear—like all parents.

But her situation was a little different. She was a virgin who was not yet married—and pregnant! The fingers were probably pointing left and right, and there was probably plenty of whispering around the corner and name calling, accusing her of being an adulteress. Add to this the fact her childhood was quickly coming to a close and she was carrying the Anointed One promised to her people for generations, and it's a wonder she didn't have a nervous breakdown!

And yet, while Mary probably felt lots of different emotions, she chose to *express* only one: joy.

She could have been angry at her situation; she could have *feared* it. But she didn't. Instead of fearing she was "ecstatic," instead of dreading the baby to come or being angry over the news, she "[overflowed] with praises to God" for what he was doing for her, for her people, and for the world!

How many of us respond in such a way when we receive news we're not entirely thrilled about or weren't expecting? What a reminder to us this Christmas season is Mary's response!

No matter what news comes our way, may we join Mary in "overflowing with praises to God." May our spirits "[burst] with joy over my life-giving God," because he has set his tender gaze upon us.

Just like he did for Mary.

Advent Prayer of Joy

Lord, no matter what comes my way, I promise to burst with joy and overflow with praise because I have been favored and blessed by you, the Mighty One! Amen.

Day 3

THE GOD WHO WORKS MIGHTY MIRACLES

(Luke 1:46–51)

There's this old American spiritual, "Go Down Moses." It describes events in the book of Exodus and relates Israel's struggle to their own struggle for freedom. Here's the first line:

> When Israel was in Egypt's land: Let my people go,
> Oppress'd so hard they could not stand,
> Let my people go.
> Go down, Moses,
> Way down in Egypt's land,
> Tell old Pharaoh,
> Let my people go!

In this song "Israel" represented the African-American slaves while "Egypt" and "Pharaoh" were symbols of their slavemasters. The slaves who sang this song were looking for a mighty miracle from the Mighty One—they were looking for a *new* Exodus to bring them to freedom.

In many ways, Mary and her people were looking and waiting for the same kind of deliverance. Remember what's happening in Mary's world: Israel was under Roman occupation; Herod was a horrible dictator who oppressed the people of Israel and taxed them out the nose; Israel was waiting for the Anointed One to come and to fight their final fight against their Roman oppressor, to drive their enemies from their land, and reestablish temple worship.

Some of this is reflected in the language that describes Mary in a "lowly" place. In her lowly state as a poor, oppressed teenager she represented all of Israel who themselves were powerless and poor.

And yet they were not without hope. Because the Mighty One scatters the proud, brings down rulers from their thrones, and sends the rich away empty.

It's no wonder she's ecstatic and bursts with joy! Because as she sings: "The Mighty One was working a mighty miracle for me…Mighty power flows from him to scatter all those who walk in pride."

Anyone listening to Mary's song would have thought Herod the Great and Rome! Mary believed that God was about to turn the tables on her oppressors and deliver her people, just like he had done in the past with the single greatest act of Israel's deliverance: The Exodus.

Psalm 136 uses this same language to speak about God's faithful deliverance: "He brought his people out of Egypt with miracles! His tender love for us, Continues on forever! With his mighty power he brought them out!" (136:11–12).

God redeemed his people from slavery, and he was about to do the same thing in a *new* Exodus through his Anointed One, the Son whom Mary was now carrying. This new exodus was better than the African-Americans' hope for release from Southern slavery and freedom in the North. This one brought release for all people from slavery to sin and death and to new-life freedom.

Advent reminds us of the coming of the Anointed One who brought with him the new Exodus, the new *deliverance*. Join with Mary in praising the Mighty One who has worked miracles of deliverance for us all!

Advent Prayer of Joy

O Mighty One, I thank you this Christmas season for working a mighty miracle for me by delivering me from the bondage of sin and death, shame and guilt! Amen.

Day 4

THE STORY ABOUT THE GREATEST REVERSAL EVER!

(Luke 1:52–53)

Stories with reversals make the best tales, don't they? We cheer for the high school nerd who gets the girl while the popular jock is left in the dust. We shout for joy when the quaint, small mountain town fends off a large New York development firm from building a ski resort. And we're happy to see the upstart political campaign win against the well-financed veteran from DC.

These kinds of stories are so great because life doesn't always turn out this way in the real world. Often it seems like the ones who win are the rich, well connected, and powerful, while the poor, defenseless, and weak suffer the consequences.

What's so great about God's story is that what rarely

happens in real life actually comes true! The lowly are lifted, the high and mighty are torn down, the proud are scattered, the hungry are filled.

By stepping into our world, God through Jesus Christ paved the way for deliverance from the wickedness that comes from the proud, mighty, and rich.

And yet, what God is revealing here through Mary's song isn't simply the demise of political dictators and fat-cat CEOs. Rather, *anyone* who does not fear God and look to him to supply their needs are in trouble.

You see, part of the problem with the mighty, the proud, and the rich is that their hope isn't in God but in *themselves*. And Mary's song warns that God is against such people—tearing them down and sending them away empty. Because only "those who hunger for [the Mighty One] will always be filled" (1:53).

The "smug and self-satisfied," however, "He will send away empty." These people are anyone who is self-sufficient and declare they need no salvation. God raises up the lowly, but the mighty want to raise up themselves. Throughout Luke's gospel, this spirit of self-exaltation is the key to sinfulness—as Proverbs 16:18 says, "The higher you lift up yourself in pride, the harder you'll fall in disgrace."

In Luke 6, Jesus speaks blessings over the lowly and the

hungry—just like in Mary's song. But to the rich and the well fed, "What sorrows await," Jesus says.

Through Mary and her "mighty miracle," God is finally delivering his people—all people—but that deliverance, mercy, and salvation only extends to those who fear him, the song says. To those who trust God and God alone for that rescue.

This season what do you need deliverance from? Are you looking to God or yourself? "Be willing to be made low before the Lord, and he will exalt you," James reminds us (4:10).

Because unlike real life, our God produces the greatest of reversals by lifting up the lowly. God the Father did so for his Son, raising him from the dead when all seemed lost; God the Son did so for you, by dying for you at just the right time when you were dead in your sins; God the Holy Spirit continues to work on our behalf, keeping his promises to Abraham's descendants forever—all of which is cause for great joy!

Advent Prayer of Joy

Lord, I praise you for being a God of reversals: a God who lifts the lowly, tears down the smug and satisfied, and fills those who hunger after you. Help me to humble myself in order to be satisfied this Christmas season. Amen.

Day 5

THE NEVER-FORGETTING, ALWAYS PROMISE-KEEPING GOD

(Luke 1:54–55)

A day doesn't go by when someone forgets the promises they made—to their employees, to the ones who elected them, to us.

A business owner promises there will be no more layoffs, and then six months later another round of your friends are sent packing. The president promises no new taxes, and two years later you're giving more of your paycheck to Uncle Sam.

Or how about something more personal: your friend promises to keep your deepest struggle to herself, yet a week later you catch wind that everyone in your circle knows what haunts you; you believe your husband's promise to stop his Internet habit once and for all, only to discover the same smutty websites back in his web browser history.

People fail us left and right, and one of the main reasons is because they forget their promises—no, they *break* their promises.

Not God, not the Mighty One!

He is the never-forgetting, always promise-keeping God. And that's something to jump up and down with joy over, isn't it?

Mary sure does. She sings about her joy because she's ecstatic, she overflows with praises to God, her spirit bursts with joy over her life-giving God. One of the reasons she sings this way is "because [the Mighty One] can never forget to show mercy, he has helped his chosen servant, Israel, keeping his promises to Abraham and to his descendants forever" (Luke 1:54–55).

Our God never forgets to show mercy. Israel had sung about this mercy for generations with several psalms, like Psalm 36:

> But you, O Lord, your mercy-seat love is limitless, reaching higher than the highest heavens. Your great faithfulness is infinite, stretching over the whole earth. Your tender care and kindness leave no one

> forgotten, not a man nor even a mouse. O God, how extravagant is your cherishing love! (Ps. 36:5-7)

For generations God had helped his chosen servant, Israel. Despite the countless times they turned their backs on him, God didn't give them what they deserved. That's enough for anyone to jump up with joy!

But God's love for his people doesn't stop there. Because not only does he never fail to show mercy, God never, never forgets. No matter how big the promise, no matter how *old* the promise, our God is the never-forgetting, always promise-keeping God. To the point of making good on a promise he gave way back to the very first of his chosen people, Abraham.

In Genesis 12, God promised to make a great nation out of Abraham; to bless those who blessed him and curse those who cursed him; to bless all peoples on the planet through him and his offspring. And Mary recognized that this was the moment God was making good on his promise—not only to the Jewish people, but to *all* peoples. Through her Son, God finally made good on his promise.

Because God is a never-forgetting, always promise-keeping God, we have forgiveness from sins, release from shame and guilt, and all the blessings of this life and the next.

If that's not reason to join with Mary this Christmas season in jumping up and down in ecstatic, overflowing, soul-bursting joy—then I don't know what is!

Advent Prayer of Joy

Never-forgetting, always promise-keeping God, I join with Mary this Advent in overflowing with praise and joy to you for your limitless mercies and for remembering your promise to rescue and restore me and my world! Amen.

Week Four

Love

Week Four

SCRIPTURE READINGS

PSALM 89:1–4, 19–26

[1] This forever-song I sing of the gentle love of God!
Young and old alike will hear about
your faithful, steadfast love—never failing!
[2] Here's my chorus: "Your mercy grows through the ages.
Your faithfulness is firm, rising up to the skies."
[3] I heard the Lord say, "My covenant has been made
and I'm committed forever to my chosen one, David.
[4] I have made my oath that there will be sons of
    David forever,
sons that are kings through every generation."

Pause in his presence

[19–20] You spoke to your prophets in visions, saying,
"I have found a mighty hero for my people.
I have chosen David as my loving servant and exalted him.

I have anointed him as king with the oil of my holiness.
[21] I will be strength to him and I will give him
my grace to sustain him no matter what comes.
[22] None of his enemies will get the best of him,
nor will the wicked one overpower him.
[23] For I will crush his every adversary
and do away with all who hate him.
[24] Because I love him and treasure him,
my faithfulness will always protect him.
I will place my great favor upon him,
and I will cause his power and fame to increase.
[25] I will set his hand over the sea
and his right hand over the rivers.
[26] And he will come before me, saying,
'You truly are my Father, my only God, and my
strong deliverer!'"

LUKE 1:67–80

Zechariah's Prophecy

[67] Then Zechariah was filled to overflowing with the Holy Spirit and he prophesied, saying:

[68] "Praise be to the exalted Lord God of Israel,
for he has seen us through eyes of grace,
and he comes as our Hero-God to set us free!

[69] He appears to us as a mighty Savior,
a trumpet of redemption from the house of David,
his servant,
[70] Just as he promised long ago
by the words of his holy prophets.
[71] They prophesied he would come one day and save us
from every one of our enemies
and from the power of those who hate us.
[72] Now he has shown us the mercy promised to
our ancestors,
for he has remembered his holy covenant.
[73–75] He has rescued us from the power of our enemies!
This fulfills the sacred oath he made with our
father Abraham.
Now we can boldly worship[d] God with holy lives,
living in purity as priests in his presence every day!
[76] And to you I prophesy, my little son,
you will be known as the prophet of the glorious God.
For you will be a forerunner,
going before the face of the Master, Yahweh,
to prepare hearts to embrace his ways.
[77] You will preach to his people the revelation of
salvation life,
the cancellation of all our sins, to bring us back to God.
[78] The splendor light of heaven's glorious sunrise
is about to break upon us in holy visitation,

all because the merciful heart of our God is so very tender.
[79] The word from heaven will come to us
with dazzling light to shine upon those
who live in darkness, near death's dark shadow.
And he will illuminate the path that leads to the way
of peace."

[80] Afterward, their son grew up and was strengthened by the Holy Spirit and he grew in his love for God. John chose to live in the lonely wilderness until the day came when he was to be displayed publicly to Israel.

Day 1

THE FAITHFUL, STEADFAST, NEVER-FAILING LOVE OF GOD

(Psalm 89:1–4, 19–26)

If you've ever watched professional sports on television you've probably seen at some point some fan hold up a big cardboard sign that read, *JOHN 3:16*—usually in big, bright, bold lettering.

One of the most famous verses ever, right? Perhaps you memorized it as a little child. Here's a reminder of its powerful message:

> "For this is how much God loved the world—he gave his one and only, unique Son as a gift. So now everyone who believes in him will never perish but experience everlasting life." (John 3:16)

For this is how much God loved the world—he gave... What a declaration! It's no wonder our bold sports fan wanted to attract attention to help people experience the amazing gift of God's amazing love.

Thousands of years ago a poet wrote some similar words—a song, actually—to broadcast far and wide to young and old the amazing love of God, just like our sports fan.

Look at how he wrote about this love: God's love is so good that it "overwhelmed" him; he described this love as "faithful," "steadfast," and "never failing;" and the chorus he sings rises to magical heights with "Your mercy grows through the ages. Your faithfulness is firm, rising up to the skies" (Ps. 89:2).

Like our sign-wielding sports fan, the poet wanted the world to know about God's love, but not just any love. A love expressed through his forever-commitment to his "chosen one, David" and "every generation" after him.

This promise ends Book III of the Psalms, which speaks of God's seeming abandonment of his people. But we know the Lord did not abandon his people, or humanity for that matter.

Because the fruit of God's promise "that there will be sons of David forever, sons that are kings through every generation" came with the ultimate Son and King of kings, Jesus. Throughout the New Testament Jesus is referred to as the Son of David, the rightful heir of David's dynasty and fulfillment of all of God's promises to his people.

The message of this psalm is the same one in John, and the one that marks this Christmas season:

God loves you; he has not abandoned you! He promised to rescue humanity, and he made good on that promise through the Son of David.

So let's stand up and join the psalmist and sing this forever-song of the gentle, overwhelming love of God!

Advent Prayer of Love

Lord God, I want what this poet wants: for young and old alike to hear about your faithful, steadfast, never-failing love. May I sing of your love forever, a love that overwhelms me! Amen.

Day 2

THE HERO-GOD WHO SAVES THE DAY

(Luke 1:67–79)

Who was your childhood hero?

Maybe it was Batman, the caped crusader who put his life on the line to fend off criminal masterminds and fight for justice.

Maybe the warrior princess of the Amazons, Wonder Woman, who similarly fought to put the world to rights—all with her Lasso of Truth and pair of indestructible bracelets.

Or perhaps your hero was less otherworldly, instead he or she was a favorite teacher, the neighborhood police officer or firefighter, or Mom or Dad.

Have you ever thought of God as a hero? The kind of God who is interested in rescuing you and putting your broken, busted world back together again?

If not, take a closer look at Zechariah's prophetic song,

because that's exactly how he viewed Yahweh, the God of Israel.

Filled with the Holy Spirit, Zechariah prophesied the Lord was *finally* coming to do what he had promised to do generations past: rescue his people from their enemies and put their world back together once and for all. He was coming to do what he had done before!

Because of his great love for his chosen people, Yahweh led them out of Egypt and through the Red Sea; the Lord went before them as the bright cloud and pillar of fire on their way to the Promised Land; and he cared for Israel during their exile and then brought them back home again. Just as the Hero-God broke into Israel's world as their mighty Savior in generations past, Zechariah prophesied the time had come for him to show up in power and might once again.

No wonder Zechariah called him their Hero-God! Because unlike the superheroes of our childhood, this God acted not out of obligation or an overinflated ego—our Hero acted with a furious, raging love.

Everyone needs a hero, someone to look up to, someone to count on to get them through seasons of drought and the darkest valleys of life.

Is God your hero, is he your Hero-God? Zechariah prophetically declared our Hero has appeared to us as "a mighty Savior, a trumpet of redemption."

From what do you long to be rescued? How do you want your world put back together again? Turn to your Hero-God this Christmas season, knowing he longs to do for you what he promised long ago—all in the name of love.

Advent Prayer of Love

God, I need a hero this Christmas season, and I know of others who need a hero too. I pray that you would be for me and for them what Zechariah prophesied—a mighty Savior, come to rescue me and put my broken, busted world back together again. Amen.

Day 3

THE LOYAL GOD WHO LOVES BY REMEMBERING US

(Luke 1:70–75)

There is a simple three-word message embedded in Zechariah's powerful, prophetic word, and it's this: God loves you.

God loves you. Read that again. Now speak it out loud, trusting that it's true—that the God of the universe *loves* you!

This kind of love isn't just any love—especially *our* kind of love. God's love is a *loyal* love, it's a *remembering* love.

Zechariah speaks about this love when he speaks of the holy prophets prophesying "He would come one day and save us from every one of our enemies and from the power of those who hate us."

That day has already arrived! God made good on his

promise and showed his people mercy by remembering his holy covenant. The mercy here is the same mercy Mary spoke of, where "[God's] mercy kisses all his godly lovers, from one generation to the next" (Luke 1:50).

This kind of mercy is what we call *covenantal loyalty*—the Hebrew word is *hesed*. This is the kind of love and loyalty a wife shows her cheating husband when he comes crawling back. It's the kind of love a parent shows his child who crashes the family car.

Throughout the Old Testament Israel is called an adulteress and a whore—because she breaks their relationship with the Lord by running after false gods and rebelling through her behavior. Yet what does God do time and time again? He takes her back. All because of his *hesed*, his *loyalty* to the relationship he created with his people.

Because God is a God of love because he is a God who *remembers*.

Zechariah says that God remembered his covenant. This theme of *covenant remembrance* is a major theme in Israel's story. In Egypt, God remembered. In the wilderness, God remembered. In Babylon, God remembered. And now under Roman occupation, God remembered.

If you think about it, *covenant remembrance* and *loyalty* is a major theme in each of *our* stories as well. Think about the times when God was loyal to you, when God loved you by remembering you by coming to you and welcoming you back.

He remembered his love for you when he came and welcomed you back.

God has remained loyal to you because God loves you, and so he has remembered you. Celebrate and praise God for that loyal, remembering love this Advent!

Advent Prayer of Love

God, thank you for loving me by remembering me and staying loyal to me—even after the countless times I have not loved you by being loyal to you and remembering you. Amen.

Day 4

HAVE YOU HEEDED THE WARNING OF JESUS' PAUL REVERE?

(Luke 1:76–77)

If you who paid any sort of attention in your high school American history class you'll recall the colonial patriot Paul Revere. He is famous for his "midnight ride" through present-day Somerville, Medford, and Arlington, Massachusetts, to warn fellow patriots of British troop movements.

While Revere probably did not shout the phrase later attributed to him—"The British are coming!"—because his mission depended on secrecy, he did announce along the way "The Regulars are coming out!" in order to warn his fellow colonists and to help key revolutionary leaders make the necessary military preparations.

Revere's mission bearing the warning of danger was a mission of love, because it saved the colonists from certain danger, preserved their lives, and helped them fend off impending British attacks.

There was another person who had a similar mission of preparation who also bore a warning of danger for the sake of preserving people's lives. We know him as John the Baptist. Look at how his father, Zechariah, prophesied about his own mission of love:

> "And to you I prophesy, my little son, you will be known as the prophet of the glorious God. For you will be a forerunner, going before the face of the Master, Yahweh, to prepare hearts to embrace his ways. You will preach to his people the revelation of salvation life, the cancellation of all our sins, to bring us back to God." (Luke 1:76–77)

Like Paul Revere, John went into the towns, making a declaration for the purpose of saving people's lives. Luke says he "went preaching and baptizing throughout the Jordan Valley. He persuaded people to turn away from their sins and turn to God for the freedom of forgiveness" (Luke 3:3).

He warned people, "turn away from your sins, turn to God, and prove it by a changed life" and "Give food to the hungry, clothe the poor, and bless the needy" (Luke 3:8, 11).

And when he was asked if he was the expected Messiah, he replied, "There is one coming who is mightier than I. He is supreme. In fact, I'm not worthy of even being his slave. I can only baptize you in this river, but he will baptize you into the Spirit of holiness and into his raging fire. He has in his hands a winnowing fork to clean up his threshing floor! He will separate the wheat from the chaff. The wheat he will gather into his barn, but he will burn the chaff in a fire that no one can ever put out!" (Luke 3:16–17)

That's some warning! And John was faithful in his mission of love to prepare the way for the One who would bring salvation, cancel all our sins, and bring us back to God.

Zechariah said his son would prepare hearts to embrace [the mighty Savior's ways]."

May you let John's message prepare your heart to make room in your life for the mighty Savior—a message of love that announces rescue, salvation, the cancellation of your sins, and the reparation of your relationship with God!

Advent Prayer of Love

Lord Jesus Christ, Son of God, I thank you for the ministry of John, who lovingly prepared the hearts of people to receive you as Savior and King. Help me make room in my life for you, my Savior, this Advent season. Amen.

DO YOU KNOW HOW MUCH GOD LOVES YOU? THIS MUCH!

(Luke 1:78–79)

Do you know how much God loves you? Take a look at the end of Zechariah's prophetic word and some of the original Greek to understand the depth of God's love:

"The splendor light of heaven's glorious sunrise is about to break upon us in holy visitation, all because of *splanchna eleou theou*" (1:78).

Zechariah speaks of a God, the holy God who made a "holy visitation" in order to rescue us and put our lives back together again, *all because of his compassionate bowels*!"

Bowels? WHAT? Yes! The original Greek is literally translated "because of the compassionate bowels of God," which

The Passion Translation expresses as "All because the merciful heart of our God is so very tender" (Luke 1:78).

In the ancient world the seat of emotions wasn't in the *heart* like it is thought of in our world. Instead the ancients believed they resided in our large intestines and colon and whatnot—in the very depth of our being.

Imagine a young man getting down on one knee and saying, "Honey, I love you with my *whole* large intestine! Will you marry me?" That's what Zechariah is saying here!

Deep within himself, God loved us so much that he sent his Son Jesus Christ to die a bloody, painful death for you and me. He did this to benefit us in two big ways:

1) So that we would no longer walk in darkness; 2) and instead walk in God's lovely peace.

We translate *shalom* peace, but it's more than that. It really means wholeness. Jesus' mission was to guide the lost, to guide those dwelling in darkness into God's loving way which leads to God's peace—to a put-back-together-again life.

During his ministry Jesus had compassion on the crowds, Mark says, because they were like sheep without a shepherd. They were wandering around lost. They didn't know how to act, and they didn't understand who God was, that they should love and worship him and him alone.

And then at the end when Jesus rode toward Jerusalem Luke says,

> When Jesus caught sight of the city, he burst into tears with uncontrollable weeping over Jerusalem, saying, "If only you could recognize that this day peace is within your reach! But you cannot see it." (Luke 19:41–42)

They didn't recognize what Zechariah recognized: humanity's Hero-God came out of a deep love to save us and bring us peace.

So this Christmas season, know this: God loves you with every ounce of his being! And celebrate the kind of mercy and light and peace that Zechariah celebrated!

Advent Prayer of Love

My holy Hero-God, thank you for breaking in upon the world in holy visitation two thousand years ago, all because of your deep, deep love for us. Amen.

SCRIPTURE READINGS

PSALM 98:1–9

[1] Go ahead—sing your brand-new song to the Lord!
He is famous for his miracles and marvels,
for he is victorious through his mighty power and
holy strength.
[2] Everyone knows how God has saved us,
for he has displayed his justice throughout history.
[3] He never forgets to show us his love and faithfulness.
How kind he has been to Israel!
All the nations know how he stands behind his people
and how he saves his own.
[4] So go ahead, everyone, and shout out your praises
with joy!
Break out of the box and let loose
with the most joyous sound of praise!

[5] Sing your melody of praise to the Lord
and make music like never before!
[6] Blow those trumpets and shofars!
Shout with joyous triumph before King Yahweh!
[7] Let the ocean's waves join in the chorus with their roaring praise
until everyone everywhere shouts out in unison,
"Glory to the Lord!"
[8] Let the rivers and streams clap with applause
as the mountains rise in a standing ovation
to join the mighty choir of exaltation.
[9] Look! Here he comes! The Lord and judge of all the earth!
He's coming to make things right and to do it fair and square.
And everyone will see that he does all things well!

LUKE 2:1–20

The Birth of Jesus

[1-2] During those days, the Roman emperor, Caesar Augustus, ordered that the first census be taken throughout his empire. (Quirinius was the governor of Syria at that time.) [3] Everyone had to travel to his or her hometown to complete the mandatory census. [4-5] So Joseph and his fiancé,

Mary, left Nazareth, a village in Galilee, and journeyed to their hometown in Judea, to the village of Bethlehem, King David's ancient home. They were required to register there, since they were both direct descendants of David. Mary was pregnant and nearly ready to give birth.

[6–7] When they arrived in Bethlehem, Mary went into labor, and there she gave birth to her firstborn son. After wrapping the newborn baby in strips of cloth, they laid him in a feeding trough since there was no available space in any upper room in the village.

An Angelic Encounter

[8] That night, in a field near Bethlehem, there were shepherds watching over their flocks. [9] Suddenly, an angel of the Lord appeared in radiant splendor before them, lighting up the field with the blazing glory of God, and the shepherds were terrified! [10] But the angel reassured them, saying, "Don't be afraid. For I have come to bring you good news, the most joyous news the world has ever heard! And it is for everyone everywhere! [11] For today in Bethlehem a rescuer was born for you. He is the Lord Yahweh, the Messiah. [12] You will recognize him by this miracle sign: You will find a baby wrapped in strips of cloth and lying in a feeding trough!"

[13] Then all at once, a vast number of glorious angels appeared, the very armies of heaven! And they all praised God, singing:

[14] "Glory to God in the highest realms of heaven!

For there is peace and a good hope given to the sons of men."

[15] When the choir of angels disappeared back to heaven, the shepherds said to one another, "Let's go! Let's hurry and find this Word that is born in Bethlehem and see for ourselves what the Lord has revealed to us." [16] So they ran into the village and found their way to Mary and Joseph. And there was the baby, lying in a feeding trough.

[17] Upon seeing this miraculous sign, the shepherds recounted what had just happened. 18 Everyone who heard the shepherds' story was astonished by what they were told.

[19] But Mary treasured all these things in her heart and often pondered what they meant.

[20] The shepherds returned to their flock, ecstatic over what had happened. They praised God and glorified him for all they had heard and seen for themselves, just like the angel had said.

Christmas Eve or Christmas Day

SHOUT FOR JOY, FOR THE MESSIAH HAS COME...AND WILL COME AGAIN!

(Psalm 98:1–9; Luke 2:1–20)

"Joy to the World" is probably the most popular and well-known of Christmas songs. It was originally written by English hymn writer Isaac Watts, and is based on Psalm 98.

If you recall the song's lyrics, you'll notice there isn't any mention of shepherds or a manger, stars or wise men—not even Mary and Joseph are mentioned! That's because Watts originally wrote the hymn not to celebrate Jesus' *first* coming, but to celebrate his second triumphant return at the end of the age.

While this may seem a little odd, it makes sense when you realize the whole point of the Advent season in the first place. The term *Advent* comes from the Latin word *adventus*, meaning "coming." During the Advent season, Christians prepare for the different "comings" of Christ—first as a baby born to take away the sins of the world, and second as the victorious King coming to put the world back together again.

In celebrating Christ's first coming, we are invited to respond as the shepherds responded.

You'll recall that one evening there were some shepherds tending their flocks at night when they received the most unexpected, exciting, amazing news. The angel of the Lord told them the long-awaited Anointed One had just been born!

After their quiet, peaceful evening was totally disrupted by this announcement, they responded in four ways: they *went*, they *saw*, they *shared*, and they *praised*.

How else could they have responded other than to get up and go? And yet so many don't. The announcement's been made, the invitation sent out to the world—to you and your family—so how have you responded?

Have you made the effort to go see this coming, like those shepherds did? Because it's only when you see and experience Jesus for yourself that you realize he is who you've been waiting for your whole life. And when you do, when you taste and see that the Lord Jesus is good, our only response is to not only follow him, but to share him too.

After the shepherds saw and experienced for themselves the gift God had given to the world, they couldn't help but blast the news of what came from every rooftop in Bethlehem.

When they did, "Everyone who heard the shepherds' story was astonished by what they were told" (Luke 2:18). In other worlds, the world was rocked! It still is every time we tell and retell and tell again that old, old story of Jesus and his love.

So this Christmas Eve and Day we are invited to respond as the shepherds did. But it doesn't end there. Because in expecting Christ's second coming, we are invited to respond as the psalmist responded too.

You can almost see a mirror image of our favorite Christmas carol in Psalm 98, can't you? We are invited to "shout our praises with joy;" to sing a new song and "make music like never before" with all kinds of instruments.

But there's more! Every corner of the world is invited to this joyous party too. Oceans are invited to "join in the chorus with their roaring praise" (Ps. 98:7). Rivers and streams are invited to "clap with applause as the mountains rise in a standing ovation" (Ps. 98:8).

Why? Why this shouting and praise, why this applause and ovation?

Because not only has the Lord *come*, the Lord is *coming!* The Lord and judge of all the earth is "coming to make things right and to do it fair and square." And when he does, "everyone will see he does all things well!" (Ps. 98:9)

On Christmas we celebrate the gift given to the world, our Rescuer, the Lord Yahweh, the Messiah. We celebrate all he taught and how he lived. We celebrate all he endured when he died. We celebrate his triumph over sin and death on the other side of the grave through the resurrection.

But, if you can imagine it, the greatest gift is yet to come! For while he wore strips of cloth and lay in a feeding trough for his first coming, on *that* day he will be wearing a white robe and riding a white horse to finally make things right—to finally put this broken, busted world back together again!

Yes, celebrate his first coming, and let's also look to his glorious one to come!

Advent Christmas Eve - Christmas Day Prayer

Almighty God, you have given your only-begotten Son to take our nature upon him, and to be born this day of a pure virgin: Grant that we, who have been born again and made your children by adoption and grace, may daily be renewed by your Holy Spirit; through our Lord Jesus Christ, to whom with you and the same Spirit be honor and glory, now and forever. Amen.

A WORD ABOUT THE PASSION TRANSLATION

It would be impossible to calculate how many lives have been changed forever by the power of the Bible, the living Word of God! To hold the Bible dear to your heart is the sacred obsession of every true follower of Jesus. Yet to go even further and truly understand the Bible is how we gain light and truth to live by. We believe God is committed to giving us truth in a package we can understand and apply, so we thank God for every translation of God's Word that we have.

God's Word does not change, but over time languages definitely do, thus the need for updated and revised translations of the Bible. Translations give us the words God spoke through his servants, but words can be poor containers for revelation because they leak! Meaning is influenced by culture, background, and many other details. Just imagine how differently the Hebrew authors of the Old Testament saw the world three thousand years ago from the way we see it today! Even within one language and culture, meanings of words change from one generation to the next.

The Passion Translation (TPT) is committed to bringing forth the potency of God's Word in relevant, contemporary vocabulary that doesn't distract from its meaning or distort it in any way. There is no such thing as a truly literal translation of the Bible, for there is not an equivalent language that perfectly conveys the meaning of the biblical text. Is it really possible to have a highly accurate and highly readable English Bible? We certainly hope so! It is so important that God's Word is living in our hearts, ringing in our ears, and burning in our souls. Transferring God's revelation from Hebrew and Greek into English is an art, not merely a linguistic science.

The "best" translation is one that makes the Word of God clear and accurate no matter how many words it takes to express it. That's the aim of The Passion Translation: to bring God's eternal truth into a highly readable heart-level expression that causes truth and love to jump out of the text and lodge inside our hearts. A desire to remain accurate to the text and a desire to communicate God's heart of passion for his people are the two driving forces behind TPT.

The purpose of The Passion Translation is to reintroduce the passion and fire of the Bible to the English reader. It doesn't merely convey the literal meaning of words. It expresses God's passion for people and his world by translating the original, life-changing message of God's Word for modern readers. We pray this version of God's Word will kindle in you a burning desire to know the heart of God, while impacting the church for years to come. Please visit ThePassionTranslation.com for more information.